GETTING A JOB IN
AUTOMOTIVE CARE
AND SERVICE

MINDY MOZER

ROSEN
PUBLISHING®

NEW YORK

Published in 2014 by The Rosen Publishing Group, Inc.
29 East 21st Street, New York, NY 10010

First Edition

Library of Congress Cataloging-in-Publication Data

Mozer, Mindy.
Getting a job in automotive care and service/by Mindy Mozer.—1st ed.—New York: Rosen, c2014
      p. cm.—(Job basics: getting the job you need)
Includes bibliographical references and index.
ISBN 978-1-4488-9609-7
1. Automobiles—Maintenance and Repair—Vocational guidance—Juvenile literature. 2. Automobile industry and trade—Vocational guidance—Juvenile literature. I. Title.
TL152.M69 2014
629.28'72023—M877

Manufactured in the United States of America

CPSIA Compliance Information: Batch #S13YA: For further information, contact Rosen Publishing, New York, New York, at 1-800-237-9932.

CONTENTS

INTRODUCTION

The automobile repair technician inspects the Chevrolet Corvette. Dressed in steel-toed boots and blue coveralls, his job is to figure out what's wrong with the car. The owner reports that the "check engine light" has been on for two days and that he feels a jarring transition when the car shifts gears. The owner also found a little fluid on his driveway. The technician pops the hood and checks the transmission fluid. It's low. He plugs in a diagnostic scan tool that tells him what is causing the check engine light to flash. The technician has confirmed that there's a problem with the transmission. He reviews the information with his supervisor and begins fixing the car.

The Corvette is one of several cars the technician will repair on this particular day, and one of dozens he will see during his workweek at a local garage. Fixing cars is what the technician has wanted to do since he took a basic automotive repair class in high school. After he graduated, he enrolled in an associate of applied science degree program at a community college. There, he took classes in subjects such as steering, alignment and suspension, manual transmissions, automatic transmissions, and engine performance. He considered getting a certificate instead so that he could enter the workforce after only one year of study after high school. Ultimately, however, he liked the idea of getting more hands-on experience in a two-year associate's program.

Auto repair technicians, also called mechanics, like to work with their hands. They can be found at a variety of businesses, from small gas stations to car dealerships. An auto repair technician is just one of many jobs in the automotive care and service industry.

After completing his degree, the future automobile repair technician began looking for a job. He searched for job openings online, networked with friends and teachers, and got some help preparing his résumé from a local job center.

His time spent preparing didn't end after he landed an interview. He researched the local garage online, prepared a list of questions to ask during the interview, and practiced answering questions that he might be asked. On the day of the interview, he put on his newly purchased dress clothes and presented himself as a confident and capable employee. After the interview, he sent thank-you notes to the employees he met with and followed up with a telephone call. Ten days later, he was offered his dream job.

The technician knows that he still has a lot to learn about fixing cars and fitting in at the business. He also has a lot to learn about managing a regular paycheck, setting goals for the future, and excelling and advancing in his career. But then he remembers that only two years ago, he knew little about getting a job in automotive care and service. He knew nothing about educational programs, how to find job openings, and preparing for interviews. That seemed overwhelming then, but by taking it one step at a time, he was able to get where he is today.

Others who like to fix and tinker with cars and trucks can also find the perfect job in the automotive care and service business by taking similar steps. They just need to invest a little time and effort in learning about the field and the process.

CHAPTER ONE

Picking the Perfect Position

Some people prefer to drive a sedan. Others like the roominess of a station wagon. Some prefer cruising in a roadster. And others like the fuel efficiency of a hybrid, which uses an electric motor as well as gasoline. Just as there are different types of brands, makes, and models of cars, there are different types of jobs in the automotive care and service industry.

Auto Repair Technician/ Mechanic

Auto repair technicians are like doctors for automobiles and trucks. A person brings in a car that isn't working right, and technicians have to figure out why and how to fix it. They have to do it quickly, meet dealer standards, and give the customer an accurate price. Most important, they need to fix the vehicle right the first time or the customer will not return for service in the future.

Auto repair technicians work at gas stations, privately owned garages, car dealerships, and large national repair companies. The technicians are also called mechanics,

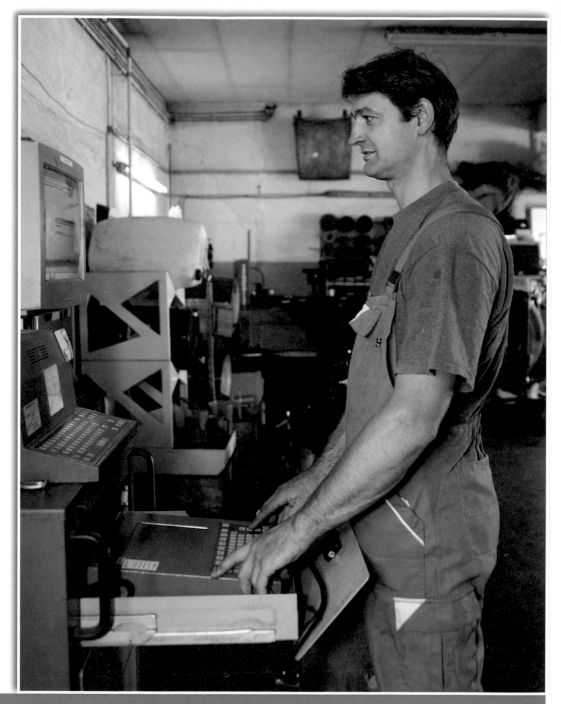

Auto repair technicians use sophisticated computerized equipment to figure out what is wrong with cars. Most garages require auto repair technicians to have at least a high school diploma and some formal training.

depending on the place of employment. The term "auto repair technician" has been used more often in recent years because cars have become more advanced over time. Auto repair technicians today use sophisticated computerized equipment to figure out what is wrong with cars. They can then make the necessary repairs, using power tools or traditional handheld tools to fix problems. The hours that auto repair technicians work vary, depending on the company. Many businesses are open on nights and weekends, which requires technicians to work those shifts. Technicians aren't worried about getting dirty. They work with their hands repairing greasy parts of a vehicle.

Oftentimes, auto repair technicians specialize in one area of car repair, such as brakes, transmission, or tune-ups. The amount of education needed for the job depends on the specialty and the place of employment. Most garages require at least a high school diploma and some formal training. The typical duties of an auto repair technician include:

- **Preventive maintenance:** Inspecting vehicles, tuning up engines, changing the oil, rotating tires, balancing wheels, and replacing filters
- **Repairs:** Fixing engine problems, replacing car parts, fixing mechanical and electrical system malfunctions, and repairing body damage
- **Vehicle upkeep:** Cleaning, washing, painting, and replacing worn parts
- **Record keeping:** Maintaining detailed records on service and repairs. This may include researching car warranties to keep costs low for customers.
- **Shop upkeep:** Ordering supplies and making sure they are received

- **Staying educated:** Reading trade journals and taking advantage of learning opportunities to stay on top of the latest advancements in car technology

Diesel Service Technicians/ Mechanics

Diesel service technicians work on vehicles that have diesel engines, which include buses and trucks. That is why they are sometimes called bus and truck mechanics. Bus mechanics may work for companies that are in charge of keeping an entire fleet operating. They make sure the buses stay in working order and are operating safely. Diesel service technicians also work on diesel-powered automobiles and boats. Diesel technicians need to be able to work with the electronic systems that are part of these big vehicles. The typical duties of a diesel service technician are similar to those of an auto repair technician and include:

- **Routine inspections:** Inspecting and adjusting brake systems, tightening bolts, aligning wheels, changing the oil, checking batteries, repairing pumps and compressors, and lubricating equipment
- **Diagnosing problems:** Attaching test instruments to equipment to find problems, listening to defective equipment, and using testing instruments like handheld computers and pressure gauges. Test-driving trucks and buses to find problems and make sure the vehicles are working properly
- **Shop upkeep:** Ordering supplies and making sure they are received

- **Staying educated:** Reading trade journals and taking advantage of learning opportunities to stay on top of the latest advancements in diesel technology

Automotive Body and Glass Repairers

Automotive body and glass repairers fix damaged bodies and body parts of automobiles, trucks, vans, trailers, and buses that have been in accidents. They restore the vehicles to the

Automotive body and glass repairers work in auto body repair shops, car dealerships, and specialized custom-refinishing businesses. One of their duties is to replace damaged windshields and window glass.

way they looked and operated before the accident. Glass repairers replace windshields and window glass. This may involve obtaining replacement windows for specific automobile makes and models from suppliers and installing them.

Automotive body and glass repairers work in auto body repair shops, car dealerships, and specialized custom refinishing businesses. Most of these workers have completed a formal training program, but some learn the skills they need on the job. The duties of an automotive body and glass repairer include:

- Estimating the cost of the repair after reviewing damage reports
- Pounding out dents, straightening frames, and welding metal parts
- Repairing or replacing fenders, bumpers, hoods, grilles, or other body parts
- Filling damaged areas with solder or plastic body fillers
- Installing and weatherproofing windows and windshields
- Realigning car chassis (the metal framework of the vehicle)
- Filing, grinding, sanding, and smoothing filled or repaired surfaces
- Refinishing with a primer coat, sanding, and painting with a finish coat
- Aiming headlights and aligning wheels

Painting and coating workers specialize in painting a vehicle. They pick out the paint, prepare the automobile for painting, and then apply the paint.

Heavy Vehicle and Mobile Equipment Service Technicians

Heavy vehicle and mobile equipment service technicians repair vehicles used in construction, farming, and other industries. These technicians fix the equipment that moves materials and helps construct buildings, such as steam shovels, cranes, and dump trucks. Farm equipment mechanics work on tractors and combines. Mobile heavy equipment mechanics repair construction equipment, such as bulldozers and excavators. Those who work for the federal government repair military equipment. Rail car repairers specialize in railroad locomotives.

Heavy vehicle and mobile equipment service technicians repair engines, hydraulic systems, and transmissions in vehicles used in farming, such as John Deere tractors.

Like other technicians, heavy vehicle technicians repair engines, hydraulic systems, transmissions, and electrical systems. They keep brakes and transmissions running smoothly.

TIPS ON FIGURING OUT THE RIGHT CAREER

•What do you do well? Write down the tasks you do well. If you figure out your natural talents and interests, your job won't feel like work.

•Whom do you admire? Make a list of the people you look up to and why.

•What makes you happy? What activities are you doing that make you happiest?

•What's your work style? Do you like to work under deadline pressure with strict guidelines, or do you prefer a flexible work schedule and environment? Which environment allows you to do your best work?

•Where do you want to work? Do you want to work for a big company or a small operation? How far away from home do you want to work? Do you want to live in a small town or a large city?

•Do you like working with others? Do you want to be part of a team? Do you like to share ideas with others and solve problems in groups, or would you rather work alone?

•Do you mind working on weekends or in the evenings? Are regular hours important to you, or can your schedule change each week?

•Do you want to work with customers? Are you good at talking to people and representing a company?

•How well do you handle stress? Do you thrive under stress, or do you prefer a laid-back job?

•How much money do you want to make? How much money do you anticipate needing in five years?

The job duties of heavy vehicle and mobile equipment service technicians include:
- Performing scheduled maintenance
- Diagnosing problems; replacing worn parts; and testing engines, hydraulics, and electrical systems
- Taking apart and reassembling heavy equipment
- Traveling to worksites to repair large equipment

Small Engine Mechanics

Small engine mechanics work on motorcycles, motorboats, and outdoor power equipment. Motorcycle mechanics specialize in motorcycles, scooters, dirt bikes, and all-terrain vehicles. Motorboat mechanics work on boat engines, propellers, and

Motorcycle mechanics fix motorcycles, scooters, dirt bikes, and all-terrain vehicles. Like auto repair technicians, they use computerized equipment to diagnose problems.

other boat equipment. Other small engine mechanics repair outdoor power equipment, such as lawnmowers, chainsaws, garden tractors, snow blowers, and snowmobiles. The typical job duties of small engine mechanics include:

- Performing routine engine maintenance
- Testing and inspecting engines for malfunctioning parts
- Repairing or replacing worn, defective, or broken parts
- Putting together and reinstalling components and engines following repairs
- Keeping records of inspections, test results, work performed, and parts used

Automotive Service Managers

Automotive service managers are the bridge between customers and technicians performing the work. It is their job to make sure the work gets done on time and according to company guidelines and that customers are satisfied. These people are strong problem solvers, communicators, listeners, and team leaders.

In some garages, technicians specialize on a certain task. For example, a technician will fix brakes on a car, while another technician will work on the same vehicle's air-conditioning

Automotive service managers are problem solvers, communicators, listeners, and team leaders. They make sure vehicles are fixed on time and that customers are satisfied.

systems. The service manager makes sure all of the necessary tasks get done on that car and the work is complete. Career opportunities at the managerial level include service writers, assistant managers, estimators, and customer service representatives. The duties of an automotive service manager include:

- Working with customers to determine what repairs are needed. This may involve questioning customers or, in some cases, driving vehicles.
- Preparing work orders showing estimated costs
- Writing a description of problems on repair orders so that the technician can locate and fix them quickly
- Explaining the work performed to customers
- Explaining the bill to customers
- Handling customer complaints

CHAPTER TWO

In the Classroom

Although it's possible to be trained on the job in the automotive care and service industry, most places of employment require some formal instruction. Formal instruction can range from a one-year certificate program to a four-year bachelor's degree program and beyond. For those who want training after high school, the best place to start is a community college or technical school. Community colleges often hold free informational sessions for prospective students that describe their degrees and programs.

High School Training

Many high schools offer basic classes in automotive repair and electrical trades. This is a great way to jump-start a career in the automotive industry. Some high schools provide on-site automotive courses, such as entry-level exploratory classes in shop fundamentals and classes where students learn job-entry skills. Schools may also partner with local community colleges. This kind of partnership allows students to receive credit at those colleges and at their high school. Some automobile dealers also offer training programs through local colleges. Other high schools have more formal service technician programs.

Many high schools offer basic classes in automotive repair. Those classes are a good way to see if a career in automotive care and service is right for you.

Although mechanics can get a job in the automotive care and service industry with just a high school degree, more are becoming certified or getting an associate's or bachelor's degree in auto repair at a community college or vocational school. One reason for this is that those who enter the workforce with an advanced degree are likely to make more money.

Certificate Programs

Auto mechanic certificate programs can usually be completed in a year or less. A high school diploma and a valid driver's license are typically required to enroll. These

Even mechanics with an associate's degree or bachelor's degree in auto repair learn on the job and rely on employees with more experience to serve as mentors.

programs are geared toward students who want to start working as soon as possible and don't want to wait several years to earn an associate's or bachelor's degree. The programs are offered at community colleges and career training schools. At the end, students leave with a certificate instead of a degree. One tradeoff of certificate programs is that because it takes less than a year to complete them and earn certification, classes move quickly and coursework isn't in-depth. Graduates aren't as experienced and knowledgeable as those with an associate's or bachelor's degree. Students can find certificate programs by looking online, talking to high school advisers, or by

FINDING A MENTOR

A mentor is a trusted counselor or guide. He or she is someone who can provide you with advice in your field or help you learn more about a business. Here are some tips on finding a mentor:

- **Check with local companies:** They might have a formal mentoring program in place that you could join.
- **Try professional organizations:** Some professional associations, community service organizations, and trade unions have mentoring programs.
- **Network with people you know:** Distant relatives and friends of the family may be able to suggest a mentor.
- **Start small:** Instead of asking someone if he or she will be your mentor, ask for advice in one area. You can then work your way into a more formal relationship.
- **Figure out what you want your mentor to help you with:** Do you want someone who can help you break into the automotive care field, or do you want someone who can help you with general business challenges, such as how to dress? A mentor does not have to be in the same field as you to provide sound career advice.
- **Take notes:** There's no point in having a mentor if you aren't going to listen to his or her advice. Ask questions and be open-minded.
- **Have fun:** Meet for lunch or an activity. Get to know your mentor, and you will get more out of the experience.
- **Say thanks:** Do something to thank your mentor.
- **Be a mentor:** Pay it forward and help somebody else when you are in a position to do so.

calling their community college. Financial aid may be available.

Students in automotive repair certificate programs learn basic mechanics and automotive care. All of the classes and workshops focus on automotive care, so students aren't required to take general courses, such as math or English. Depending on the program, students may have the opportunity to focus on one area, such as brake repair or auto electrical systems. Graduates of certificate programs leave knowing how to diagnose and fix basic engine problems, complete repair and maintenance paperwork, use appropriate tools, and work on a team. Classes can include engine performance, basic car maintenance, electrical systems, air conditioning and heating, suspension and alignment, transmissions, manual drive trains, brake systems, automatic drive trains, and fuel control systems. Students get some hands-on garage experience. Graduates of certificate programs find work as air-conditioning repairers, tune-up technicians, front-end mechanics, and brake specialists.

Associate's Degrees

The next level of education is an associate of applied science (AAS) degree. Students in associate's degree programs take classes in automotive care as well as general education classes. Students who finish this degree, which takes about two years, are qualified for entry-level positions. Students must have a high school diploma and a valid driver's license to enroll in classes. Many of these programs require students to provide their own toolkits for hands-on activities. These kits can cost thousands of dollars, but some programs help with financial aid.

Some community colleges work with car companies to offer specialized training programs. General Motors offers the General Motors Automotive Service Education Program. This is a two-year program that includes college instruction and on-the-job training at a GM dealership. Graduates earn

Some community colleges work with car companies to offer specialized training programs. The General Motors program takes two years and includes college instruction and on-the-job training.

associate's degrees in automotive technology. Buick, Cadillac, Chevrolet, GMC, and ACDelco Professional Service Centers also often sponsor students. The Toyota/Lexus Technical Educational Network offers a similar two-year program that alternates college instruction with on-the-job training at a Toyota/Lexus dealership.

Students in associate's degree programs take classes such as steering, alignment and suspension, manual transmissions, automatic transmissions, and engine performance.

An associate's degree also prepares students for the exam required to achieve the Automotive Service Excellence (ASE) certification. Many businesses require their workers to have this certification. The National Institute for Automotive Service Excellence grants this certification. The ASE provides more than forty certifications in automobile repair, from brakes to diesel engines. To get this certification, a technician has to pass a series of tests and have at least two years of work experience.

Bachelor's Degrees

A student who wants more training gets a bachelor's degree in automotive maintenance and technology. This typically takes about four years to complete, but some programs can be completed in three years, depending on the number of classes a student takes each year. Other students who take a light load of classes may take six years to finish the program. Schools may require students to have certain grade point averages and standardized test scores before admitting them. Students may also have to complete an interview to be accepted into the program.

Students in these programs take general maintenance classes. However, they can also take management and business courses if, for instance, they are interested in becoming managers. Students may learn about spreadsheets, automotive technology, alternative fuels, hydraulics, marketing, and human relations in these classes. These programs may also require internships during which students can get hands-on experience in the field. Graduates of these programs start in higher-level jobs, such as fleet supervisors and facility managers.

FINDING AN AUTOMOTIVE PROGRAM THAT IS RIGHT FOR YOU

- Get recommendations from current and past students for a particular program.
- Research all scholarships and grants that are available. Check with the school's finance department about financial aid.
- Ask the school how many of its graduates get jobs and where those jobs are located.
- Factor in the cost of books, supplies, and tools that you will need for your classes.
- Visit a local garage and find out where the employees received their training.
- Attend an informational session so that you can pick the program that suits your needs.
- Ask if you can visit a classroom or laboratory so that you can get a sense of what is involved before enrolling.

Master's Degrees

A master's degree is a degree that a person gets after a bachelor's degree. These programs go beyond auto repair and may concentrate on automotive engineering, electronics, or business administration. People with these degrees may work for automotive research companies, regulatory organizations, or government laboratories.

Internships, Work-Study, and Cooperative Education Programs

The best way to learn is by doing. Internships are one way to get real-world experience. An internship can be paid or can be for school credit, depending on the company and the program. Even if the internships are paid positions, interns won't make much money. Instead, they will get experience that will help them land a job down the road. Interns work beside regular employees and learn by doing. They also get a sense of what the work environment is like. And when it comes time to find a full-time job, interns have professional references for their résumé and contacts in their field.

Students in postsecondary (after high school graduation) education programs may qualify for work-study programs. These are programs in which students earn money for tuition by working at pre-approved places. Students must qualify for these programs, which are based on financial need. More information on these programs is available at college financial aid or work-study offices.

Cooperative education programs, also called co-ops, allow students to get work experience in between classroom experience. Students in co-op programs take a break from their classes and generally work full-time in their field. This gives them the chance to work on bigger and longer-term projects. Co-ops also help students figure out the part of the job in which they want to specialize. Universities that offer co-op programs help students identify the best educational and professional opportunities available.

Internships and co-op programs help students get real-world experience in automotive care and service. These students work beside regular employees and learn by doing.

Online Programs and Continuing Education

There are online automotive technician certificate programs available. With online programs, students take classes and exams on the Internet. The advantage of these programs is that students don't have to travel to take classes. The disadvantage is that they require more independent study. Check to make sure the school and online program are accredited before enrolling.

The learning doesn't end after securing a job. The technology in automobiles is always changing, and those in the automotive care and service industry must keep up with those changes. Local colleges, dealerships, and garages offer workshops and training opportunities to employees to keep their skills and expertise as current as possible.

CHAPTER THREE

Finding a Job

Searching for work can be a full-time job in itself. Finding a job doesn't usually happen quickly. It takes patience, research, and effort. The first task is to get an understanding of the type of jobs available in the area. A good way to start seeing what is out there is to search for job openings online. Those without computers can visit local libraries and community centers, where computers with Internet access are often available to visitors.

When starting a job search, it's good to become familiar with the work options available in the local area. Many businesses have Web sites that list the range of automotive services they offer, business histories, and staff profiles. Candidates can read about these businesses to see if they fit their needs and goals before applying for jobs.

Employment Web Sites

There are large employment Web sites online, such as CareerBuilder.com and Monster.com, which list thousands of job openings across the country. On these Web sites, people can search for jobs with keywords, by category, or by location of the business. For example, typing in "automotive technician" creates a list of automotive technician jobs available throughout the country. Each entry provides more information about

A good first step when searching for a job is to get an understanding of what is available both locally and nationally. This can be done online, where large employment Web sites list thousands of job openings.

the job, whether it is part-time or full-time, its requirements, and how to apply. To narrow down a job search, type in a geographic location. Continue searching for job openings by changing the keywords to see the range of positions available. These Web sites also provide career advice, help writing résumés, and links to resource articles.

Other Web sites also allow visitors to zero in on job openings in their communities. Craigslist.com, for example, offers free classified advertisements listing everything from lawnmowers for sale to job openings. Employment Web sites can come and go, so another method of surveying the field is to do an online search for a specific job title. This will also provide a good indication of the type and number of jobs available in the area. In addition, professional associations may post job openings across the country on their Web sites. Even nonmembers of the organization can apply for jobs listed on these job boards.

Be sure to watch out for scams when searching for jobs online. If a job sounds too good to be true—offers a high salary, work from home, flexible hours—it often is. Job postings that are legitimate will never ask for Social Security numbers, birth dates, bank account information, or credit card information.

Social Media

Employers are now using social media to advertise job openings and search for job candidates. Social media provides a way for people to interact online. This includes everything from Web sites, such as Facebook, to blogs and Internet forums. There is one important thing to remember about using social media to find a job: just as users can get information about businesses, businesses can get information about potential employees. Always be careful about the personal information you post online. Every time you post something on Facebook, for example, remember that others can read it, including your parents and grandparents, prospective employers, and future in-laws. Think before you post!

Some examples of social media that are often used by employers and job seekers alike include:

- LinkedIn, a social network primarily aimed at people in the business world. Users can make a professional profile, list places they have worked, and connect with

Social networking sites, such as Facebook (www.facebook.com), provide a way for people to interact online. They also allow users to get information about businesses, and businesses to get information about future employees.

colleagues. LinkedIn has a search engine that connects users to jobs and includes a job board that lists people at specific companies whom users may know.

• Twitter, which allows users to send and receive messages, called tweets. Tweets are up to 140 characters in length and are delivered to people who "follow" the author. Along with sending them, users can read tweets sent by those people they have followed. Many companies send tweets about their latest news, products, services, and job openings.

• Facebook, a social networking site that allows users to create personal profiles and exchange information with friends. Users can also join common-interest groups and "like" potential employers' pages or professional associations. Some companies will mention job openings in their Facebook updates.

- Blogs, online information sites with entries displayed in reverse chronological order. They provide commentary or news on specific subjects. Blogs are usually interactive, so readers can add their opinions. They can include photos and links to other Web pages.

FINDING A GOOD PLACE TO WORK

Here are some things to look for when trying to determine if a business is a good place to work:

1. Employees are generally happy.
2. The business has an efficient workflow.
3. Current and past employees recommend working at this business.
4. Employees have confidence in the owner or manager.
5. Employees believe the business is headed in the right direction.
6. Pay is fair for the work performed.
7. Employees are confident about the future of the business.
8. The business has good values and a strong work ethic.
9. Employees feel appreciated.
10. Employees have opportunities to learn, try new things, and advance.
11. The business offers a competitive benefits package.
12. There's flexibility when an employee's work and personal life need to be balanced.
13. Managers are easy to communicate with and support their employees.
14. The opinions of employees are respected.
15. The business follows proper safety procedures.

Job Centers and Job Fairs

Job centers help people figure out what job or career is best for them, search for job openings, create a résumé, and apply for job openings. Job centers also help businesses recruit workers and provide training. They are generally free, and many offer walk-in hours. People meet with career advisers at these centers to develop an action plan. The career adviser will direct people to resources and help them check job openings online.

A job or career fair is a good way to meet with potential employers in a particular area. Job fairs are usually held at convention centers or hotels. Local universities, colleges, and community colleges also sponsor job fairs that may be open to the public. Company representatives can provide information

Company representatives often provide information about employment opportunities at job fairs, where they hand out brochures and answer questions about their businesses.

about their workplace and direct those interested to any current or future job openings. Job fairs are also good opportunities to learn more about a company than what is available online.

Job fairs can be loud and overwhelming, so participants need to be prepared. Here are some ways to make the most of a job fair:

1. Be patient. Expect to wait in long lines. Wear comfortable shoes.

2. Dress appropriately. A job fair is like a job interview, so dress professionally. Attendees should style their hair conservatively. Women should wear little makeup.

3. Bring résumés. Have a supply of résumés to give to company representatives.

4. Prepare an elevator speech (see sidebar) that summarizes your experience and career goals.

5. Be prepared. Attendees should be ready to talk in-depth about the type of job they want, their education, their skills, and where they see themselves in five years.

6. Arrive early. This allows participants to park, check in, and scope out businesses that they would like to learn more about.

7. Network. Talk to other job candidates while waiting in line. Another candidate may be able to provide tips about job openings or other career fairs in the area.

8. Show initiative. Participants should introduce themselves to recruiters. Shake their hands. Smile.

9. Ask questions. Be sure to prepare at least three questions about each company.

10. Stay positive. Don't be concerned about the many applicants talking to employers. Participants should not worry if they do not land a job. Job fairs are good

CRAFTING AN ELEVATOR SPEECH

An "elevator speech" is a short description of a product, person, service, or organization. The term was coined because the speech should last no longer than a typical elevator ride—no more than about two minutes. Salespeople pitching their products to potential customers often use an elevator speech. But it can also work when networking and looking for a job. In the job-seeking version of the elevator speech, a person focuses on why he or she should be hired. Here's how to write an elevator speech:

1. Write down your top five experiences related to the position you are hoping to land. This can include your education, internships, or other work experience. With each experience, explain the situation, what you did, and the end result.
2. Edit each experience down to one paragraph.
3. Think about the themes in each experience. What does each experience say about you?
4. Pick the top themes that you want people to remember about you.
5. Write down your immediate goals.
6. Combine information about who you are with your future goals in a speech that is no more than 250 words.
7. Practice your pitch.

opportunities to practice interviewing skills, meet new people, and explore the available options.

Using Connections

Networking is a good way to find out about job openings and land a job. Businesses get dozens of résumés when they have a job opening. Managers are more likely to hire someone they

Job fair participants need to come prepared with a supply of résumés and a short speech that summarizes their experiences and career goals.

know or someone who is recommended by someone they know. That is why it is important to establish a network of people in the field.

Start with friends and relatives. Ask people if they know of someone working in the automotive industry. Use contacts made in high school or college. Attend professional meetings, conferences, or conventions. Talk to people in religious groups or other social and community groups. Chat with neighbors. Talk to people while waiting in line at the grocery store or doctor's office. Volunteer in the community to meet new people.

CHAPTER FOUR

Fueling Up for the Interview

Landing a job interview starts with a strong résumé. A résumé is a description of your skills, education, and work experience. It highlights your achievements and shows employers that you are qualified for the job. It's important to create a clear and concise résumé because potential employers will often make snap judgments about whether or not you are qualified after reading it quickly. Here's how to put together a résumé. Start by brainstorming in the following way:

1. Make a list of accomplishments. List work experience, volunteer experience, extracurricular activities, leadership roles, and education.
2. Write a paragraph about each item on the list.
3. Select the items to include on your résumé. You should pick the items that will demonstrate to potential employers that you are capable of doing the job.

Putting It All Together

When putting the résumé together, draw upon your brainstorming notes and follow this sample outline:

When putting together a résumé, make sure there are no spelling or grammatical errors. Applicants should craft a different résumé tailored specifically to each job opening.

- Name and Address
- Objective – An objective shows an employer the type of job you are hoping to find. Listing it is optional: it should not be included if you don't have a clear goal in mind. Make sure the objective matches the job for which you are applying. Use direct language and be specific. Here is a sample objective: "To obtain an auto technician position in which I can use my associate of applied science degree and expertise in brake repair."
- Education – List the highest level of education you have obtained first. For example, if you have an associate of applied science degree, list that at the top, followed by high school. Include a grade point average if it is above a 3.0. You can highlight specific courses you studied if they are relevant to the job. List any honors and awards received in school. If you don't have a degree or certificate yet, list the date you expect to get it.
- Experience – This section should highlight paid work experience, but it can also include any unpaid internships

and volunteer work if they are relevant to the job. Refer to your list of accomplishments when writing this section.

• Activities – This is an optional section if you have activities that show you are qualified for the job. Include interesting hobbies or extracurricular clubs that relate to the job and might help you stand out.

• Reference List — You should be sure to create a list of three to five people who can speak positively about your work habits and skills. Potential employers will likely contact these people, so you must ask them in advance about being a reference before listing their names. List references on a separate page. Include each person's name, title, company, work address, phone number, and e-mail address. Bring the list to the interview.

Résumé Writing Tips

• Make sure there are no spelling or grammatical errors. Read the résumé at least twice and ask a friend or relative to review it as well.

• Make sure the font is big enough to read. Don't use anything under 12 points.

• Applicants should not include pictures of themselves, birth dates, or Social Security numbers.

• Tailor each résumé to the specific job for which you are applying. The résumé should emphasize the skills that an applicant has for that specific position.

• Tell the truth. Applicants should never exaggerate their experience or skills.

• A résumé should be no longer than two pages. One page is better.

TOP 10 RÉSUMÉ WRITING MISTAKES

1. **Spelling errors and typos.** Your résumé creates a first impression of you to prospective employers. If your grammar and spelling aren't perfect, a recruiter will think that you don't care, are lazy, or can't write. Make sure you have someone else read your résumé because it is easy to miss your own mistakes.

2. **Lack of specifics.** Tell employers what you have accomplished. For example, instead of writing, "Worked in a garage repairing cars," say, "Worked in a 10-person garage repairing five vehicles a day, specializing in break repair."

3. **Too long.** A one-page résumé is preferred for people just entering the workforce.

4. **Disorganized.** Make sure your résumé is easy to follow and read. Use a consistent style with each entry. Use one font throughout the document.

5. **Generic.** Make sure your résumé is written specifically for each job, highlighting why you would fit into that specific business. If your résumé is vague or generic, you likely won't get an interview.

6. **Too much personal information.** Do not include information about your religious background, marital status, age, or race.

7. **No cover letter.** A cover letter is your official introduction to the business. Your résumé won't make sense without it. Make sure a cover letter is conversational and doesn't just repeat the content of the résumé.

8. **Highlights duties instead of accomplishments.** Emphasize what you accomplished instead of what you were simply assigned to do.

9. **Incorrect contact information.** Double-check to make sure your e-mail address, street address, and phone number are all correct.

10. **Writing in complete sentences.** Instead of writing complete sentences in the résumé, use bullets to quickly explain your accomplishments. Avoid clichés and overstatements. Don't say you have "excellent communication skills" without offering examples to back up that claim.

- Use a good printer and print the résumé on white or light paper.
- Do not use pronouns, such as "I" or "me" when writing the résumé.

Cover Letter

A cover letter is typically sent with each résumé. The goal of the cover letter is to catch the attention of recruiters or employers so that they look at the accompanying résumé. A cover letter can also add a personal touch to a résumé. Cover letters tell recruiters why you are interested in the company while also highlighting your skills.

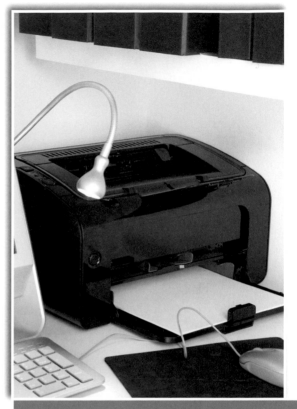

Job applicants should print a résumé on white or light paper with a good printer. A cover letter also helps applicants stand out.

There are three types of cover letters. The application cover letter is sent for a specific job opening. The cover letter should be written specifically for the open position. A prospecting letter asks for information about possible job openings. A networking letter asks for career advice or help with a job search.

Here is how a cover letter should be formatted when applying for a specific job:

Your name
Address
Phone number
E-mail address

Date

Employee name (if available)
Title (if available)
Company
Address

Dear Mr./Ms. Last Name,

The first paragraph should explain why you are writing. If applying for a specific job, name the job. Include how you found out about the open position if it was through networking.

Next, describe why you should be considered for the job. Do not repeat your résumé word for word. Instead, you should summarize your qualifications in a conversational format.

End the letter by thanking the recruiter for considering you for the job and include information on how you will follow up.

Sincerely,

Your signature

Your typed name

Preparing for the Interview

Now that you have your résumé and cover letter together, you have to prepare for the interview. After all the hard work that job seekers put into getting the interview, they sometimes feel they are done once they get one. But just as much work and preparation must go into the interview itself as went into the seeking of the interview. Preparing thoroughly for a job interview can make the difference between getting the job of your dreams and losing out to someone who seemed like a better candidate because he or she prepared and interviewed well.

Research the Company

The first thing to do is learn everything about the company before going to the interview. Find out how many employees it has and the products and services it offers. Learn about the history of the company, when it

A strong job applicant researches a company, including its history and the products and services it offers, before the interview.

started, and who is and has been in charge. Be prepared to answer the questions, "What do you know about this

A job applicant should dress conservatively for a job interview. He should look at himself in the mirror before leaving his house to make sure all buttons are buttoned and zippers are up.

company?" "What do you think about this company?" "Are there areas in which this company can improve?"

You can get information about a company online. Google the name to find its Web site. Read any news articles that may have been written about the company. Then create a list of questions to ask about it. You should find out who you will be meeting with during the interview and memorize their names and job titles.

Practice

Make a list of your skills and then practice talking about them. Be prepared with answers to questions such as, "Why are you interested in this position?" "What are your strengths? What are your weaknesses?" "Why should we hire you?" "Tell me about yourself."

Clothes

Dress conservatively and wear clothes that have been ironed. A good rule of thumb is to dress one step above how employees at the business are dressed. Be well groomed with clean, manicured nails. Wear little jewelry and makeup. Avoid using fragrances. Remove any facial piercings and cover all visible tattoos. First impressions are important.

What to Bring

Bring at least two copies of your résumé and reference list. Bring a pen and notebook and a list of questions about the business.

Arrival

Be ten to fifteen minutes early. Applicants should make sure they know where they are going. Depending on the location, they might want to practice driving there and finding parking (or taking public transportation) a few days before the interview. Although it's good to be early, don't arrive more than fifteen minutes early. The company may not be ready for you if you arrive thirty minutes ahead of the scheduled interview.

CHAPTER FIVE

Nailing the Interview

G etting a job interview is only half the battle. The key to doing well at a job interview is creating a good first impression. Making a good first impression starts even before the interview begins.

• **Check appearances:** Look at yourself in a mirror to make sure food isn't stuck in your teeth and there aren't any stains on your shirt. Straighten ties and check to make sure all buttons are buttoned and zippers are up.

• **Waiting for the interview:** Act professionally while waiting for the interviewer to meet you in the lobby, office, or conference room. Don't bite your nails, twirl your hair, or play with your clothing. You shouldn't talk or text on your cell phone. Put all personal items away.

• **Use the waiting time wisely:** Double-check the names and titles of the people you are meeting and how to pronounce them. Be respectful to the office manager or secretary. First impressions are important here as well.

• **Job application:** If given a job application, fill it out neatly and completely. Make sure it is accurate.

• **Greeting:** Firmly shake the interviewer's hand. A firm handshake will make you appear confident. Stand up before shaking the interviewer's hand. Never remain seated. Smile. Use a courtesy title ("Mr." or "Ms.") before the interviewer's name, and thank the interviewer for

Some job candidates will be given a job application to fill out during an interview. They should make sure all the information is accurate and their writing is legible.

the opportunity: "Hello, Mr. Smith. Thank you for taking the time to meet with me today."

• **Posture:** Don't sit down until the interviewer offers a chair. Sit comfortably, but don't look too casual. Sit up straight. Don't turn away from the interviewer or avoid eye contact.

During the Interview

Be enthusiastic and confident. Speak in a medium voice— loud enough for the interviewer to hear, but not too loud.

Applicants who speak too softly may be seen as lacking confidence. Try to avoid using slang and saying "like" and "um" repeatedly. Make eye contact with the interviewer as much as possible. Be yourself. Part of what the recruiter is determining is if you will fit into a particular workplace. A recruiter can tell when a person is faking it.

Leave the coffee in the waiting room. Or better yet, don't bring any food or drinks to the interview. Do not chew gum. Do not smoke before the interview or during the interview. Employers can get a negative impression when an applicant smells like cigarette smoke. Be sure to brush your teeth and use mouthwash.

Sell, sell, and sell: it's important for you to make yourself memorable. To do that, don't give yes or no answers to questions, and don't just read from your résumé. Talk about your achievements and what you learned from those experiences. Provide details and anecdotes that will stand out for the interviewer. Be honest; don't lie about your accomplishments or education.

Be positive. Don't say anything that could be perceived as negative about the business or current or past employees who work there. Avoid talking about controversial subjects. Also don't say anything negative about your own past employers or coworkers. Use your research to ask solid questions. Don't leave the interview without asking at least one question. Be sure to listen to the answers to your questions and follow up with other questions when necessary.

Leave specifics for later. Don't ask about the salary, vacation, and health care benefits during the interview. Those can be addressed after the job offer is made. Get the business card of each person with whom you interview. You are going

A firm handshake makes a job applicant appear confident. It's important for job applicants to make themselves memorable by talking about their achievements and staying positive.

to write thank-you notes later, and this is a good way to keep track of the people you talked to and their titles. Have extra copies of your résumé and cover letter available to hand out to the interviewer and anyone else you may meet.

Find out what's next. Before leaving, ask the interviewer what's next in the job hiring process. Will top candidates be invited back? When do they hope to fill the position? You want to show that you are interested in the job and working for this company. Be enthusiastic. Let the interviewer know you are serious—and seriously interested in working there!

TOP 10 THINGS NOT TO SAY DURING AN INTERVIEW

1. "Sorry I'm late."
2. "How much does the job pay?"
3. "How much time do I get for lunch or vacation?"
4. "What does this company do?"
5. "I have no weaknesses."
6. "I don't have any questions."
7. "I didn't like my boss at my old job."
8. "I don't have any experience."
9. "Let me tell you my life story."
10. "I only have an hour for this interview because I have to meet a friend for lunch."

TOP 10 THINGS TO SAY DURING AN INTERVIEW

1. "I am a team player."
2. "I am familiar with your business."
3. "I am flexible."
4. "My goal is to become an expert in my field."
5. "I work well with people."
6. "I am open to advice and suggestions."
7. "My goals five years from now are…"
8. "At school I learned…"
9. "I am looking for a new challenge that will allow me to use my skills."
10. "This job is a perfect match for my skills."

After the Interview

When the interview is over, that doesn't mean an applicant's job is done. Here is what you need to do:

- **Take notes:** Write down information about the company that you learned during the interview. That way, you can refer to your notes if you are asked questions later. This is also helpful if you have multiple job interviews during a short period of time.
- **Follow-up:** Be sure to follow up with any requests made at the interview. For example, if the interviewer asks for additional references, you should send them by

Job applicants should never leave a job interview without asking at least one question. They then need to listen to the answers and follow up with other questions when appropriate.

the day you said you would. If you are asked to call in a week, be sure to call.

- **Send a thank-you note:** Thank each person you met with during the interview within three business days after the interview. Be specific. If one employee gave you a tour of the business, thank him or her for showing you around. If a manager gave you important information about the job, thank the manager for the information. A thank-you note is a nice reminder that you are still interested in the job, that you take initiative, and that you are gracious and polite. Notes can be handwritten, typed, or e-mailed, depending on how the interviewer prefers receiving correspondence. If you have bad handwriting, send a typed note. Thank-you notes should be brief. Use proper spelling and grammar. Have a friend or relative read the note to check for typos.
- **Call:** Experts say to wait at least one week before calling to check on the status of a position. Wait long enough for the interviewer to have new information to tell you. If you call too soon, you could create a negative impression. Ask whether the position has been filled and whether you are still being considered for the job.

What If You're Not Hired?

Be patient. You aren't always going to get the first job you interview for. Ask for advice. You may want to ask the recruiter what you can do better the next time you interview for a job or what was missing on your résumé. Keep a good relationship with the company. A similar position may open down the road, and you want the company to think highly of you. You should still send thank-you notes, even if you are rejected immediately.

CHAPTER SIX

Making the Most of Your New Job

New employees can be buried in paperwork the first week on the job. There are health insurance and retirement plan forms to fill out. Emergency contact information needs to be provided. In some cases, identification cards are made. And there is a lot to learn about the work environment.

Insurance

Most employers, depending on the number of employees, offer some type of health insurance. There are three types of health insurance plans. Health maintenance organizations (HMOs) require people to use doctors in a specific network. Preferred provider organizations (PPOs) allow patients to use doctors in and out of the network, but out-of-network doctors cost more. Point-of-service (POS) plans are a combination of both. These plans require users to choose a doctor within the network and get a referral from that doctor before seeing a specialist both within and outside of the network. When selecting the right plan, here are some things to think about:

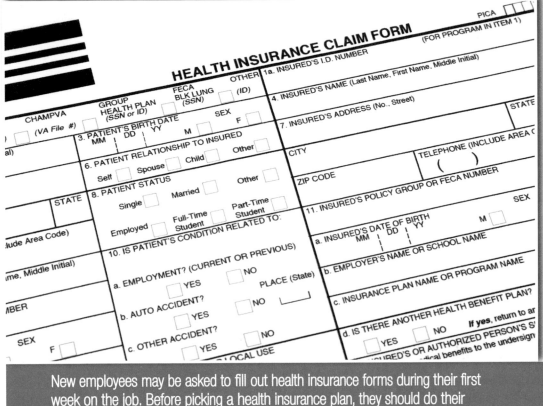

New employees may be asked to fill out health insurance forms during their first week on the job. Before picking a health insurance plan, they should do their homework and think about their current and future medical needs.

- **Medical needs:** Anticipate medical needs. People should know how much they spend each month on medication, physicals, and other medical supplies. Although they don't know if they will experience a sudden medical problem and need emergency care, they may know if they plan on starting a family soon. Those who are planning to have kids should look for a policy that includes maternity coverage.

- **Deductible:** If workers are healthy, they should think about picking an insurance policy with a high deductible. A

MANAGING MONEY

1. Set goals. Write down a list of financial goals and expectations during the next year and the next three years. For example, save $2,000 toward a car.

2. Figure out monthly income. How much money is available to you each month after taxes?

3. Figure out expenses. Make a list of monthly expenses, including rent/mortgage, credit card bills, food, and utilities.

4. Calculate discretionary spending. Figure out your flexible expenses that vary from month to month, such as restaurant meals, clothing, and entertainment.

5. Figure out quarterly or annual expenses. Examples include car insurance and taxes.

6. Create a budget. Make sure expenses are less than income. If they aren't, figure out a way to reduce expenses.

7. Save. Set aside as much money as possible each month. A guideline is to create an emergency fund that will cover three to six months of living expenses.

8. Review the budget. Look at the budget each year and make sure it is still meeting goals and expectations.

deductible is the amount a person pays out-of-pocket before insurance benefits begin. High deductible policies have cheaper monthly rates.

• **Doctors:** Make sure specific doctors are included under the plan. People usually have to pay more if a doctor is out of the insurance policy's network.

• **Out-of-pocket payments:** Some policies require you to pay a certain amount of your own money once you go over a pre-set spending limit. Make sure you are comfortable with that limit. If you have a medical emergency, out-of-pocket policies could cost a lot of money.

- **Prescription drugs:** Check which medications are covered under each option.
- **Pre-existing conditions:** People with pre-existing conditions, or known health problems, should make sure they are covered by the insurance plan.
- **Emergency care:** Plans vary regarding what is considered an emergency and how much is covered. Check to see how an emergency is defined and how much insurance covers.
- **Routine care:** Some insurance plans cover physicals, well-child visits, and other health care screenings, but some don't. Compare the plans offered to see what works best.
- **Do the math:** Figure out how much the deductibles will be before the insurance pays for your care. Look at how much the health care plan will pay after the deductible is met. Then factor in copayments for doctor visits that can be anticipated. See which plan is the best.

Retirement Savings Plans

Along with health insurance, some employers offer an opportunity for employees to save for retirement. A 401(k) is a type of retirement plan that allows employees to have a portion of their wages directly paid into an account. Before picking a plan, it's a good idea to talk to someone in human resources who can explain how the plans work.

Employees decide how much to save for retirement. They do that by telling an employer what percentage of their salary they want automatically taken out of their paycheck. This amount can be changed during the year. The money is usually taken out before the employer takes out taxes. That means employees pay taxes on a smaller salary so that their taxes are lower. Some

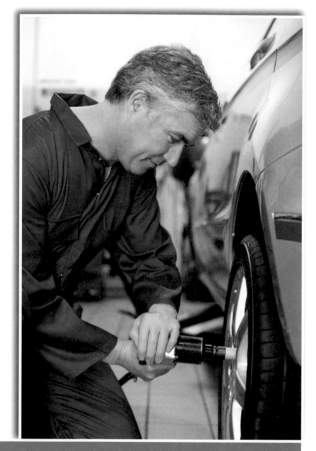

A good way to learn on the job is to watch seasoned employees—observe how they dress, their work ethic, and how they interact with managers.

employers may match a portion of the contribution, especially in 401(k) plans. In this case, try to contribute at least up to the amount the employer will match.

The money then grows in a tax-deferred plan. That means employees don't pay taxes on the money until they use it. If employees withdraw the money early, they may pay a penalty and the sum will be taxed as income. Depending on the retirement plan, workers may be able to borrow money from it and pay themselves back the amount, plus interest.

Retirement may seem like a long way off for someone who is young. But the earlier you start saving, the better prepared you will be for your future.

Learning the Workplace Culture

Businesses have certain expectations. Some employers expect employees to show a lot of initiative and are demanding. Others have strict rules about lunch breaks and hours. It's the job of a new employee to figure out what those expectations are and adapt to them. Here are some things to think about when approaching your first week of work at a new job:

- **Figure out the rules:** Ask someone in human resources if there is a written set of expectations. Find out what is expected for regarding lunch and other breaks. Clarify expectations.
- **Interaction:** Even with a written set of expectations, employees will have to figure out some rules on their own. For example, some companies may frown

After the first week, it is important for workers to show they are reliable and team players. The best employees work well with others and do what they say they are going to do.

upon conversation among workers during slow periods. Watch coworkers and follow their example.

• **Working with the boss:** See how coworkers treat the person in charge. Some bosses consider themselves to be part of the team and want to be treated as a regular employee. Other bosses set themselves apart and may require an appointment to talk to them.

• **Dress code:** Dress like your coworkers and as required by management.

• **Coworkers:** Some companies want coworkers to be competitive. Others prefer a team-building atmosphere. Either way, get to know other employees, but avoid getting involved in office gossip or cliques.

• **Workload:** Keep an eye on the work pace of fellow employees. A new employee doesn't want to start off working too quickly or too slowly.

• **Keep opinions quiet:** Don't talk about religion, politics, or other controversial and sensitive subjects. Don't suggest complete overhauls on how to work more efficiently during the first week. Building trust takes time. A new employee should get established before suggesting new ideas.

Beyond the First Day

Once a new employee has figured out the workplace culture, it is time to become a valuable member of the team.

• **Stay positive:** No one likes working with someone who is negative and constantly bringing others

New employees who show a desire and willingness to learn and be instructed will quickly find acceptance and respect in the workplace. They will also learn a lot more and do so a lot more quickly than people who think they already know it all.

down. Look on the bright side. Turn problems into challenges.

• **Learn:** Be the worker who wants to try new things and learn new skills. Don't be afraid to fail. Bosses will recognize initiative when it comes time to grant pay raises.

• **Be reliable:** Become the worker who gets the job done—every time. The best employees do what they say they are going to do and do it well.

• **Follow the rules:** Follow the written and unwritten rules of the workplace. That includes everything from dressing appropriately to getting along with coworkers.

• **Be professional:** An employee should always display the best behavior with customers. Remember the advice for a job interview—smile, make eye contact, and be self-confident. Remember one bad interaction with a customer can damage an employee's reputation in the automobile care and service field. If you have to deal with an unhappy customer, stay calm. Always validate a customer's concern by repeating the problem back to that customer. If you can't fix the problem, find someone who can. If you don't know the answer to a customer's question, be honest and tell the customer you don't know. Then find someone who does.

Acing Your Annual Review

Doing well on an annual performance review means being consistent in your work habits, attitude, and results throughout the year. Know what to expect. Make sure to understand how the business handles reviews. If a form is filled out, get a copy of that form. Find out if the business requires or encourages employees to complete a self-evaluation.

Keep records. Make notes throughout the year about work performed. Note accomplishments, failures, how those failures were fixed, and what they taught you. Track any new ideas implemented to see how those ideas helped the business. Save feedback. If a customer writes a note praising your work, save it and refer to it in a self-evaluation.

Make a list of goals for the past year and note how they were accomplished. Then make a list of goals for the

It's never too early to think about an annual performance review. Employees who do well in their reviews demonstrate consistent work habits, have a positive attitude, and produce results throughout the year.

upcoming year and a list for five years down the road. Make sure the boss knows about promotions and new positions that you are interested in. Employees should tell the boss about new skills that they would like to learn and how knowing those skills will help the company. Listen to what managers say. Don't be defensive. Don't be afraid to ask questions.

GLOSSARY

associate's degree A degree earned upon completion of a two-year program offered at a community college. It is sometimes the first two years of a four-year degree program.

bachelor's degree A degree earned upon completion of an undergraduate program at a community college, college, or university. A bachelor's degree typically takes four years.

blog An online journal. It often allows visitors to make comments on and share links from the site.

certificate program A one-year program offered at a community college or career training school. Students learn the basics about a job and get a certificate, not a degree, at the end.

cover letter A letter of introduction attached to a résumé.

deductible The initial amount that people with insurance pay when they make a claim under their insurance policies. The amount is based on the terms of the policies.

elevator speech A brief overview of a product, service, person, or organization. The term was coined because an elevator speech should be no longer than the time it takes to ride an elevator, between thirty seconds and two minutes.

Facebook A social networking service that allows users to create personal profiles, add other users as friends, and exchange messages, photos, and videos. Users can also join interest groups organized by workplace, school, or college, for example.

401(k) A retirement savings plan that allows employees to have a portion of their wages directly paid into an account. Some employers match employee contributions.

health maintenance organization (HMO) Group insurance that entitles members to the services of participating hospitals, clinics, and physicians.

internship A program of supervised training in an area or field.

LinkedIn A social networking site mainly used for professional networking. Users maintain a list of people whom they know in the business world, along with their contact information.

master's degree A degree awarded to students who finish at least one year of school after obtaining a bachelor's degree.

mentor A trusted counselor who can provide career advice.

out-of-pocket Describing a specified amount that people with insurance are expected to pay with their own money during the terms of their insurance policies. These are medical expenses that are not covered by the insurance company. The amount varies according to the specific insurance policy.

point-of-service (POS) plan A medical insurance plan that combines characteristics of both an HMO and PPO.

pre-existing condition A health problem that a person already has and is aware of when he or she applies for insurance.

preferred provider organization (PPO) A medical insurance plan in which members receive more coverage if they choose health care providers approved by the plan.

résumé A document for use during a job search that provides a quick summary of a person's skills, education, and abilities.

Twitter A social networking site that allows users to send, read, and share short messages called tweets.

Alliance of Automotive Service Providers (AASP)
1730 New Brighton Boulevard, #170
Minneapolis, MN 55413
(612) 270-6696
Web site: http://www.autoserviceproviders.com
This national association representing the automotive
    service industry in the United States was founded in
    1999. It works to strengthen its state and regional
    affiliates by promoting common business interests,
    forging strategic alliances, and monitoring federal
    legislation and regulations.

Association of International Automobile Manufacturers of
    Canada (AIAMC)
2 Bloor Street West, Suite 1804, Box 5
Toronto, ON M4W 3E2
Canada
(416) 595-8251
Web site: http://www.aiamc.com
The AIAMC represents members engaged in the manu-
    facturing, importation, distribution, and servicing of
    light-duty vehicles. It works with governments on issues
    such as vehicle safety and environmental standards
    developed by federal and provincial governments;
    reducing barriers to international trade in vehicles,
    primarily tariffs; and legal and consumer protection
    legislation, primarily at the provincial level.

Auto Careers Today
8400 Westpark Drive, #2
McLean, VA 22012
Web site: http://www.autocareerstoday.net
This is a coalition of all major automobile manufacturers
and dealer organizations. It works to promote a better
understanding of the retail side of the auto industry
and build stronger customer relationships through
shared research and development programs.

Automotive Industries Association of Canada (AIA)
1272 Wellington Street
West Ottawa, ON K1Y 3A7
Canada
(800) 808-2920
Web site: http://www.aiacanada.com
AIA is a national trade association representing the
automotive aftermarket industry in Canada. The industry is composed of companies that manufacture,
distribute, and install automotive replacement parts,
accessories, tools, and equipment. Its mandate is to
promote, educate, and represent members in all areas
that impact the growth and prosperity of the industry.

Automotive Youth Educational Systems (AYES)
101 Blue Seal Drive, S.E., Suite 101
Leesburg, VA 20175
(703) 669-6677

Web site: https://www.ayes.org

This is a partnership among participating automotive manufacturers, dealerships, and select secondary automotive programs. It is designed to encourage young people to consider careers in retail automotive service and prepare them for entry-level career positions or advanced studies in automotive technology.

Institute for Women Auto Mechanics
244 Fifth Avenue, #G205
New York, NY 10001-7604
(917) 254-1772
Web site: http://theinstitute4womenautomechanics.com

The Institute for Women Auto Mechanics introduces women to the world of auto mechanics. Among other things, it teaches women how to prevent costly automotive breakdowns and save money by doing their own auto repairs.

International Automotive Technicians Network (iATN)
640 West Lambert Road
Brea, CA 92821
(714) 257-1335
Web site: http://www.iatn.net

This is the largest network of automotive repair professionals in the world. Members of this group exchange technical knowledge with their peers around the globe.

National Institute for Automotive Service Excellence (ASE)
101 Blue Seal Drive, S.E., Suite 101
Leesburg, VA 20175
(703) 669-6600
Web site: http://www.ase.com
This nonprofit institute works to improve the quality of
vehicle repair and service by testing and certifying
automotive professionals. More than 350,000
professionals hold ASE certifications and work in
every part of the automotive service industry.

Web Sites

Due to the changing nature of Internet links, Rosen Publishing
has developed an online list of Web sites related to the sub-
ject of this book. This site is updated regularly. Please use this
link to access the list:

http://www.rosenlinks.com/JOBS/Auto

Adler, Oscar. *Sell Yourself in Any Interview: Use Proven Sales Techniques to Land Your Dream Job.* New York, NY: McGraw-Hill, 2009.

Brand, Paul. *How to Repair Your Car.* Minneapolis, MN: MBI Publishing, 2006.

Candela, Tony. *Automotive Wiring and Electrical Systems.* North Branch, MN: CarTech, 2009.

Duffy, James E. *Modern Automotive Technology.* Tinley Park, IL: Goodheart-Willcox, 2009.

Erjavec, Jack. *Automotive Technology: A Systems Approach.* Clifton Park, NY: Delmar Cengage Learning, 2009.

Gross, Ken. *Art of the Hot Rod.* Minneapolis, MN: MBI Publishing, 2008.

Gunnell, John. *How to Restore Automotive Trim and Hardware* (Motorbooks Workshop). Minneapolis, MN: MBI Publishing, 2009.

Linde, Arvid. *How Your Car Works: Your Guide to the Components & Systems of Modern Cars, Including Hybrid & Electric Vehicles.* Dorchester, England: Arvid Linde and Veloce Publishing, 2011.

Logan, Joseph. *Seven Simple Steps to Landing Your First Job.* Boulder, CO: Maytown Press, 2010.

Magliozzi, Tom, and Ray Magliozzi. *Ask Click and Clack: Answers from Car Talk.* San Francisco, CA: Chronicle Books, 2008.

Martin, Tracy. *How to Use Automotive Diagnostic Scanners* (Motorbooks Workshop). Minneapolis, MN: MBI Publishing, 2007.

Orr, Tamra B. *A Career as an Auto Mechanic* (Essential Careers). New York, NY: Rosen Publishing Group, 2010.

Palazzolo, Joseph. *High Performance Differentials, Axles & Drivelines*. North Branch, MN: CarTech, 2009.

Parks, Dennis W. *The Complete Guide to Auto Body Repair* (Motorbooks Workshop). Minneapolis, MN: Motorbooks, 2008.

Pierce, Lawrence E. *The Art of Fixing Things: Principles of Machines and How to Repair Them: 150 Tips and Tricks to Make Things Last Longer and Save You Money.* Hornby Island, BC, Canada: Lawrence E. Pierce, 2011.

Ramsey, Dan, and Judy Ramsey. *Teach Yourself VISUALLY Car Care & Maintenance*. Hoboken, NJ: Wiley, 2009.

Sclar, Deanna. *Auto Repair for Dummies*. 2nd ed. Hoboken, NJ: Wiley, 2009.

Stalder, Erika. *In the Driver's Seat: A Girl's Guide to Her First Car*. San Francisco, CA: Zest Books, 2009.

Thompson, Lisa. *Pop the Hood: Have You Got What It Takes to Be an Auto Technician?* Minneapolis, MN: Compass Point Books, 2008.

Townsend, John. *Cars and Motorcycles* (Sci-Hi: Science and Technology). Chicago, IL: Heinemann-Raintree, 2001.

Zurschmeide, Jeffrey. *How to Design, Build & Equip Your Auto Workshop on a Budget*. North Branch, MN: S-A Design, 2011.

Auto Mechanics World. "Going to Auto Mechanic School Part Two: Certificate Programs." Retrieved August 2012 (http://automechanicsworld.com/going-to-auto-mechanic-school-part-two-certificate-programs).

Borg, Kevin L. *Auto Mechanics: Technology and Expertise in Twentieth-Century America* (Studies in Industry and Society). Baltimore, MD: Johns Hopkins University Press, 2007.

Bureau of Labor Statistics. "Automotive Body and Glass Repairers." *Occupational Outlook Handbook*, March 29, 2012. Retrieved July 2012 (http://www.bls.gov/ooh/installation-maintenance-and-repair/automotive-body-and-glass-repairers.htm).

Bureau of Labor Statistics. "Automotive Service Technicians and Mechanics." *Occupational Outlook Handbook*, June 26, 2012. Retrieved July 2012 (http://www.bls.gov/ooh/installation-maintenance-and-repair/automotive-service-technicians-and-mechanics.htm).

Bureau of Labor Statistics. "Diesel Service Technicians." *Occupational Outlook Handbook*, March 29, 2012. Retrieved July 2012 (http://www.bls.gov/ooh/installation-maintenance-and-repair/diesel-service-technicians-and-mechanics.htm).

Bureau of Labor Statistics. "Heavy Vehicle and Mobile Equipment Service Technicians." *Occupational Outlook Handbook*, July 18, 2012. Retrieved July 2012 (http://www.bls.gov/ooh/installation-maintenance-and-repair

/heavy-vehicle-and-mobile-equipment-service-
technicians.htm).

Bureau of Labor Statistics. "Painting and Coating Workers."
Occupational Outlook Handbook, April 17, 2012.
Retrieved July 2012 (http://www.bls.gov/ooh/production/
painting-and-coating-workers.htm).

CAGT Exam Secrets Test Prep Team. *Certified Auto Glass
Technician Exam Secrets Study Guide.* Beaumont, TX:
Mometrix Media LLC, 2009.

Duffy, James E. *Auto Body Repair Technology.* Florence,
KY: Delmar Cengage Learning, 2008.

Education-Portal.com "Automotive Mechanics." Retrieved
August 2012 (http://education-portal.com/directory/
category/Mechanic_and_Repair_Technologies/Vehicle_
Repair_and_Maintenance/Automotive_Mechanics.html).

Hannon, Kerry. "How to Find a Mentor." *Forbes*, October
31, 2011. Retrieved August 2012 (http://www.forbes.com/
sites/kerryhannon/2011/10/31/how-to-find-a-mentor).

Investopedia.com. "7 Things You Should Say in an
Interview." April 20, 2010. Retrieved August 2012 (http://
www.investopedia.com/financial-edge/0410/7-Things-
You-Should-Say-In-An-Interview.aspx#axzz1yGDALbcE).

Johnson, Megan, and Steve Sternberg. "8 Keys to
Picking the Best Individual Health Policy." *U.S. News
& World Report*, August 7, 2012. Retrieved August
2012 (http://health.usnews.com/health-news/health
-insurance/articles/2012/08/07/8-keys-to-picking
-the-best-individual-health-insurance-policy).

Knowles, Don. *Automotive Technician Certification Test Preparation Manual*. 3rd ed. Florence, KY: Delmar Cengage Learning, 2007.

Princeton Review. "Career: Auto Mechanic." 2012. Retrieved July 2012 (http://www.princetonreview.com/careers.aspx?cid=18).

Stockel, Martin T., and Chris Johanson. *Auto Fundamentals*. Tinley Park, IL: Goodheart-Willcox, 2005.

Streufert, Billie. "Job Search 2.0: Using Facebook to Find a Job." *USA Today*, July 26, 2011. Retrieved August 2012 (http://www.usatodayeducate.com/staging/index.php/blog/job-search-2-0-using-facebook-to-find-a-job).

Thomas, Alfred M., and Michael Jund. *Collision Repair and Refinishing: A Fundamental Course for Technicians.* Florence, KY: Delmar Cengage Learning, 2009.

Tyrell-Smith, Tim. "How to Choose a Career That's Best for You." *U.S. News & World Report*, December 6, 2010. Retrieved August 2012 (http://money.usnews.com/money/blogs/outside-voices-careers/2010/12/06/how-to-choose-a-career-thats-best-for-you).

Uhrina, Paul, and James E. Duffy. *Auto Body Repair Technology.* 4th ed. Florence, KY: Delmar Cengage Learning, 2003.

Wahlgren, Kara. "Auto Repair Technician: Job Market." CollegeSurfing.com. Retrieved July 2012 (http://www.collegesurfing.com/content/article/auto-repair-technician-jobs/8598).

INDEX

About the Author

Mindy Mozer is a writer and editor living in Rochester, New York, with her husband and two children. She has written numerous books on career building and educational opportunities.

Photo Credits

Cover, p. 1 © iStockphoto.com.londoneye; cover (background), interior graphics p. 5 Blend Images/Tanya Constantine/ Getty Images; p. 8 Westend61/Getty Images; pp. 11, 28–29 iStockphoto/Thinkstock; pp. 13, 35 Bloomberg/Getty Images; p. 15 Jacques LOIC/Photononstop/Getty Images; pp. 16–17 Creatas/Thinkstock; p. 20 Spencer Grant/Photolibrary/ Getty Images; p. 21 Jetta Productions/Iconica/Getty Images; p. 24 © Southeast Community College; p. 31 Monkey Business Images/Shutterstock.com; p. 33 Dan Kitwood/ Getty Images; p. 38 Mark Ralston/AFP/Getty Images; p. 40 Image Source/Getty Images; p. 43 Jason Cox/Shutterstock .com; p. 45 Yuri Arcurs/Shutterstock.com; p. 46 Kalle Singer/ Getty Images; p. 50 Daniel Grill/Getty Images; p. 52 David Lees/Digital Vision/Getty Images; p. 54 Tim Kitchen/The Image Bank/Getty Images; p. 57 Keith Bell/Shutterstock .com; pp. 60, 61 Clerkenwell/The Agency Collection/Getty Images; p. 63 Image Source/Getty Images; p. 65 Kzenon/ Shutterstock.com.

Designer: Nicole Russo; Photo Researcher: Marty Levick